POEMS ON
THE UNDERGROUND
95

POEMS
ON THE
UNDERGROUND
95

edited by
Gerard Benson
Judith Chernaik
Cicely Herbert

CASSELL

Cassell Publishers Limited
Wellington House, 125 Strand
London WC2R 0BB

First published 1995

British Library Cataloguing in Publication Data
A catalogue record for this book is available from the British Library

ISBN 0–304–34775–2

Typeset in Monophoto Meridien by
August Filmsetting, Haydock, St Helens

Printed and bound in Great Britain by
Hillmans Printers Ltd

CONTENTS

THE POEMS

displayed on the London Underground
during 1995

Do Not Go Gentle Into That Good Night

Do not go gentle into that good night,
Old age should burn and rave at close of day;
Rage, rage against the dying of the light.

Though wise men at their end know dark is right,
Because their words had forked no lightning they
Do not go gentle into that good night.

Good men, the last wave by, crying how bright
Their frail deeds might have danced in a green bay,
Rage, rage against the dying of the light.

Wild men who caught and sang the sun in flight,
And learn, too late, they grieved it on its way,
Do not go gentle into that good night.

Grave men, near death, who see with blinding sight
Blind eyes could blaze like meteors and be gay,
Rage, rage against the dying of the light.

And you, my father, there on the sad height,
Curse, bless, me now with your fierce tears, I pray.
Do not go gentle into that good night.
Rage, rage against the dying of the light.

DYLAN THOMAS (1914–53)

'Let my shadow disappear into yours'

Låt min skugga försvinna i din.
Låt mig förlora mig själv
under de stora träden.
De som själva förlorar sin krona i skymningen,
överlämnar sig åt himmelen och natten.

Let my shadow disappear into yours.
Let me lose myself
under the tall trees,
that themselves lose their crowns in the twilight,
surrendering themselves to the sky and the night.

PÄR LAGERKVIST (1891–1974)
translated by W. H. AUDEN *and* LEIF SJÖBERG

'Now winter nights enlarge'

Now winter nights enlarge
   The number of their hours,
And clouds their storms discharge
   Upon the airy towers.
Let now the chimneys blaze,
   And cups o'erflow with wine:
Let well-tun'd words amaze
   With harmony divine.
Now yellow waxen lights
   Shall wait on honey Love,
While youthful Revels, Masks, and Courtly sights,
   Sleep's leaden spells remove.

This time doth well dispense
   With lovers' long discourse;
Much speech hath some defence,
   Though beauty no remorse.
All do not all things well;
   Some measures comely tread;
Some knotted Riddles tell;
   Some Poems smoothly read.
The Summer hath his joys,
   And Winter his delights;
Though Love and all his pleasures are but toys,
   They shorten tedious nights.

THOMAS CAMPION (1567–1620)

Look at all those monkeys

Look at all those monkeys
Jumping in their cage.
Why don't they all go out to work
And earn a decent wage?

> *How can you say such silly things,*
> *And you a son of mine?*
> *Imagine monkeys travelling on*
> *The Morden–Edgware line!*

But what about the Pekinese!
They have an allocation.
'Don't travel during Peke hour',
It says on every station.

> *My Gosh, you're right, my clever boy,*
> *I never thought of that!*
> And so they left the monkey house,
> While an elephant raised his hat.

SPIKE MILLIGAN (b. 1918)

Look at all those monkeys   Drawing by the author, in *Silly Verse for Kids*,
© Spike Milligan, by permission of Spike Milligan Productions.

Mysteries

At night, I do not know who I am
when I dream, when I am sleeping.

Awakened, I hold my breath and listen:
a thumbnail scratches the other side of the wall.

At midday, I enter a sunlit room
to observe the lamplight on for no reason.

I should know by now that few octaves can be heard,
that a vision dies from being too long stared at;

that the whole of recorded history even
is but a little gossip in a great silence;

that a magnesium flash cannot illumine,
for one single moment, the invisible.

I do not complain. I start with the visible
and am startled by the visible.

DANNIE ABSE (b. 1923)

Rooms

Though I love this travelling life and yearn
like ships docked, I long
for rooms to open with my bare hands,
and there discover the wonderful, say
a ship's prow rearing, and a ladder
of rope thrown down.
Though young, I'm weary:
I'm all rooms at present, all doors
fastened against me;
but once admitted start craving
and swell for a fine, listing ocean-going prow
no man in creation can build me.

KATHLEEN JAMIE (b. 1962)

The Good Morrow

I wonder, by my troth, what thou and I
Did, till we loved; were we not weaned till then,
But sucked on country pleasures, childishly?
Or snorted we in the Seven Sleepers' den?
'Twas so; but this, all pleasures fancies be.
If ever any beauty I did see,
Which I desired, and got, 'twas but a dream of thee.

And now good morrow to our waking souls,
Which watch not one another out of fear;
For love, all love of other sights controls,
And makes one little room, an everywhere.
Let sea-discoverers to new worlds have gone,
Let maps to others, worlds on worlds have shown,
Let us possess our world; each hath one, and is one.

My face in thine eye, thine in mine appears,
And true plain hearts do in the faces rest;
Where can we find two better hemispheres,
Without sharp North, without declining West?
Whatever dies, was not mixed equally;
If our two loves be one, or thou and I
Love so alike that none do slacken, none can die.

JOHN DONNE (1572–1631)

from Requiem

The hour of remembrance has drawn close again.
I see you, hear you, feel you:

the one they could hardly get to the window,
the one who no longer walks on this earth,

the one who shook her beautiful head,
and said: 'Coming here is like coming home.'

I would like to name them all but they took away
the list and there's no way of finding them.

For them I have woven a wide shroud
from the humble words I heard among them.

I remember them always, everywhere,
I will never forget them, whatever comes.

ANNA AKHMATOVA (1889–1966)
translated by RICHARD McKANE

The Leader

I wanna be the leader
I wanna be the leader
Can I be the leader?
Can I? I can?
Promise? Promise?
Yippee, I'm the leader
I'm the leader

OK what shall we do?

ROGER McGOUGH (b. 1937)

Adlestrop

Yes, I remember Adlestrop —
At least the name. One afternoon
Of heat, the express train drew up there
~~against its custom~~. It was June.

The steam hissed. Someone cleared his throat.
No one left & no one came
On the bare platform. What I saw
Was Adlestrop. only the name,

And, willows, willow-herb & grass,
And meadowsweet. The haycocks dry
Were not less still & lonely fair
Than the high clouds ~~that~~ in the sky.

And all that minute a blackbird sang
Close by, and round him, mistier,
Farther r further, all the birds
Of Oxfordshire r Gloucestershire.

Yes, I remember Adlestrop —
The name, because ~~of~~. One afternoon
Of heat, the express train drew up the
Unwontedly. It was late June.

Adlestrop Autograph copy, with corrections. BL Add MS 44990, f.10r.
By permission of The British Library Board.

Adlestrop

Yes. I remember Adlestrop –
The name, because one afternoon
Of heat the express-train drew up there
Unwontedly. It was late June.

The steam hissed. Someone cleared his throat.
No one left and no one came
On the bare platform. What I saw
Was Adlestrop – only the name

And willows, willow-herb, and grass,
And meadowsweet, and haycocks dry,
No whit less still and lonely fair
Than the high cloudlets in the sky.

And for that minute a blackbird sang
Close by, and round him, mistier,
Farther and farther, all the birds
Of Oxfordshire and Gloucestershire.

EDWARD THOMAS (1878–1917)

The Exiles

(translated from the author's own Gaelic)

The many ships that left our country
with white wings for Canada.
They are like handkerchiefs in our memories
and the brine like tears
and in their masts sailors singing
like birds on branches.
That sea of May running in such blue,
a moon at night, a sun at daytime,
and the moon like a yellow fruit,
like a plate on a wall
to which they raise their hands
like a silver magnet
with piercing rays
streaming into the heart.

IAIN CRICHTON SMITH (b. 1928)

Moonwise
(for my children, all)

sometimes
you know
the moon
is not such a perfect
circle

and the master Painter
makes a passing
brush touch
with a cloud

don't worry
we've passed
the dark side

all you children
rest easy now

we are born

moonwise

JEAN 'BINTA' BREEZE (b. 1956)

'My true love hath my heart and I have his'

My true love hath my heart and I have his,
By just exchange one for the other given.
I hold his dear, and mine he cannot miss,
There never was a better bargain driven.
    My true love hath my heart and I have his.

His heart in me keeps me and him in one,
My heart in him his thoughts and senses guides:
He loves my heart, for once it was his own,
I cherish his because in me it bides.
    My true love hath my heart, and I have his.

SIR PHILIP SIDNEY (1554–86)

Acquainted with the Night

I have been one acquainted with the night.
I have walked out in rain – and back in rain.
I have outwalked the furthest city light.

I have looked down the saddest city lane.
I have passed by the watchman on his beat
And dropped my eyes, unwilling to explain.

I have stood still and stopped the sound of feet
When far away an interrupted cry
Came over houses from another street,

But not to call me back or say good-by;
And further still at an unearthly height
One luminary clock against the sky

Proclaimed the time was neither wrong nor right.
I have been one acquainted with the night.

ROBERT FROST (1874–1963)

The Underground.

Summoned by Bells *The Underground* by Hugh Casson, from *The Illustrated Summoned by Bells*, with paintings and sketches by Hugh Casson (John Murray 1989). By permission of the artist. © Hugh Casson 1989.

from Summoned by Bells

Great was my joy with London at my feet –
All London mine, five shillings in my hand
And not expected back till after tea!
Great was our joy, Ronald Hughes Wright's and mine,
To travel by the Underground all day
Between the rush hours, so that very soon
There was no station, north to Finsbury Park,
To Barking eastwards, Clapham Common south,
No temporary platform in the west
Among the Actons and the Ealings, where
We had not once alighted. Metroland
Beckoned us out to lanes in beechy Bucks –
Goldschmidt and Howland (in a wooden hut
Beside the station): 'Most attractive sites
Ripe for development'; Charrington's for coal;
And not far off the neo-Tudor shops.

JOHN BETJEMAN (1906–84)

A Glass of Water

Here is a glass of water from my well.
It tastes of rock and root and earth and rain;
It is the best I have, my only spell,
And it is cold, and better than champagne.
Perhaps someone will pass this house one day
To drink, and be restored, and go his way,
Someone in dark confusion as I was
When I drank down cold water in a glass,
Drank a transparent health to keep me sane,
After the bitter mood had gone again.

MAY SARTON (1912–95)

Wind

This is the wind, the wind in a field of corn.
Great crowds are fleeing from a major disaster
Down the long valleys, the green swaying wadis,
Down through the beautiful catastrophe of wind.

Families, tribes, nations and their livestock
Have heard something, seen something. An expectation
Or a gigantic misunderstanding has swept over the hilltop
Bending the ear of the hedgerow with stories of fire and sword.

I saw a thousand years pass in two seconds.
Land was lost, languages rose and divided.
This lord went east and found safety.
His brother sought Africa and a dish of aloes.

Centuries, minutes later, one might ask
How the hilt of a sword wandered so far from the smithy.
And somewhere they will sing: 'Like chaff we were borne
In the wind.' This is the wind in a field of corn.

JAMES FENTON (b. 1949)

Season of Mists and mellow fruitfulness
  Close bosom friend of the maturing sun;
Conspiring with him how to load and bless
  The Vines with fruit that round the thatch eves run
    To bend with apples the mossed Cottage trees
      And fill all fruits with ripeness to the core
        To swell the gourd, and plump the hazle shells
  With a white kernel; to set budding more
    And still more later flowers for the bees
      Until they think warm days will never cease
        For Summer has o'erbrimm'd their clammy cells.

To Autumn   Autograph copy. By permission of the Harvard College Library.

from To Autumn

Season of mists and mellow fruitfulness,
  Close bosom-friend of the maturing sun;
Conspiring with him how to load and bless
  With fruit the vines that round the thatch-eves run;
To bend with apples the moss'd cottage-trees,
  And fill all fruit with ripeness to the core;
    To swell the gourd, and plump the hazel shells
With a sweet kernel; to set budding more,
  And still more, later flowers for the bees,
  Until they think warm days will never cease,
    For Summer has o'er-brimm'd their clammy cells.

JOHN KEATS (1795–1821)

NOTES TO THE POEMS

10 **'Let my shadow disappear into yours'**   Our contribution to an exchange of poems with Stockholm Transport, which displayed Kipling's 'A Dead Statesman' at the same time, as part of a series of poems by Nobel prizewinners.

16 *from* **Requiem**   For seventeen months, the Russian poet Anna Akhmatova queued daily outside the prison in Leningrad where her son was held. This extract from *Requiem* is part of a cycle of poems that covers the years between 1935 and 1940 and commemorates the sufferings of ordinary men and women, victims of Stalin's purges.

17 **The Leader**   This poem was first displayed on the Underground in 1989; it soon became a general favourite in school playgrounds and executive boardrooms.

20 **The Exiles**   From the time of the Highland Clearances until the early years of this century, famine and bitter poverty drove thousands of Highlanders to leave Scotland and emigrate to North America in search of a living. Iain Crichton Smith told us that the starting point for this poem was a visit he made to Canada, when he discovered many familiar Scottish place names.

22 **'My true love hath my heart and I have his'**   This famous lyric was first printed in this form by George Puttenham, *The Arte of English Poesie* (1589). Puttenham quotes the poem as an example of 'musicall ditties to be song to the lute or harpe', which suggests that it may have been set to music before 1589. The poem is a shortened version of a sonnet in Book Three of Sidney's *Arcadia*, written for his young sister, Mary, Countess of Pembroke, when Sidney was in his early twenties.

ACKNOWLEDGEMENTS

Dannie Abse: 'Mysteries' from *Selected Poems,* © Dannie Abse 1994. Reprinted by permission of Century Hutchinson.

Anna Akhmatova: 'Requiem' from *Selected Poems*, translation © Richard McKane 1989. Reprinted by permission of Bloodaxe Books.

John Betjeman: 'Summoned by Bells' © John Betjeman 1960. Reprinted by permission of John Murray.

Jean 'Binta' Breeze: 'Moonwise' from *Spring Cleaning,* © Jean 'Binta' Breeze 1992. Reprinted by permission of Virago Press.

James Fenton: 'Wind' from *The Memory of War, and Children in Exile,* © James Fenton 1983. Reprinted by permission of Penguin Books.

Robert Frost: 'Acquainted with the Night' from *The Poetry of Robert Frost* (1971). © Robert Frost. Reprinted by permission of Jonathan Cape.

Kathleen Jamie: 'Rooms' from *The Queen of Sheba,* © Kathleen Jamie 1994. Reprinted by permission of Bloodaxe Books.

Pär Lagerkvist: 'Let my shadow disappear into yours', translation by W. H. Auden and Leif Sjöberg, © Wayne State University Press 1975. Reprinted by permission of Wayne State University Press and Bengt Lagerkvist.

Roger McGough: 'The Leader' from *Sky in the Pie* (Kestrel), © Roger McGough 1983. Reprinted by permission of Peters, Fraser & Dunlop.

May Sarton: 'A Glass of Water' from *Selected Poems,* © May Sarton 1978. Reprinted by permission of W. W. Norton.

Iain Crichton Smith: 'The Exiles' from *Selected Poems,* © Iain Crichton Smith 1985. Reprinted by permission of Carcanet Press.

A NOTE OF THANKS

'Poems on the Underground' wish to thank London Underground Ltd, London Arts Board, the British Council and the Stefan Zweig Programme of The British Library.

The posters of poems displayed on the Underground during 1995, and in earlier years, can be purchased from the London Transport Museum, Freepost, Covent Garden, London WC2E 7BB.